Anonymous

Christmas-Tide Carols

First Series

Anonymous

Christmas-Tide Carols
First Series

ISBN/EAN: 9783348085809

Printed in Europe, USA, Canada, Australia, Japan

Cover: Foto ©Thomas Meinert / pixelio.de

More available books at **www.hansebooks.com**

HRISTMAS-TIDE AROLS

(*FIRST SERIES*)

THE WORDS BY

Rev. BERNARD REYNOLDS

PREBENDARY OF S PAUL'S

THE MUSIC

(Old Breton Melodies)

HARMONIZED BY

GEORGE C. MARTIN

ORGANIST OF S. PAUL'S CATHEDRAL.

Price ~~Sixpence~~ Eightpence,
WORDS ONLY, THREEHALFPENCE.

London: NOVELLO AND COMPANY, Limited.
New York: THE H. W. GRAY CO., Sole Agents for the U.S.A.

Copyright, 1891, by Novello, Ewer and Co.

Hail! Christmas Bells.

CHRISTMAS EVE.

2.

Erst on this night the Virgin holy,
   Sought shelter kind in David's town ;
Tired were her feet and wandering slowly,
   Where may she lay her burden down ?
   Where may she lay her burden down ?

3.

Kings were her sires of God anointed,
   Room for the maid of royal kin !
What home for her hath been appointed ?
   'Tis but a cave beneath an inn,
   'Tis but a cave beneath an inn.

4.

Cold was the world's unkindly greeting,
   Whilst angels flood the night with song :
Choir unto choir God's praise repeating,
   Born upon earth to right all wrong,
   Born upon earth to right all wrong.

5.

Praises with them mankind is blending,
   Praises on Christmas Eve we sing,
Praise let us give to Christ unending,
   Praise with the angel host our King,
   Praise with the angel host our King.

O'er her Child the Virgin weeps.

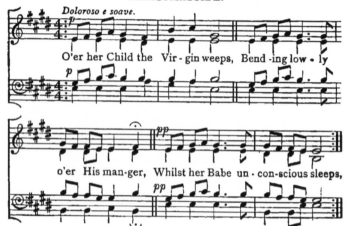

Doloroso e soave.

O'er her Child the Vir - gin weeps, Bend -ing low - ly o'er His man-ger, Whilst her Babe un - con-scious sleeps,

She her faithful vigil keeps,
    She will guard her Son from danger,
'Though her heart with anguish leaps.

2 Tears are falling o'er His head,
    Mother's tears of all the dearest;
Hands she claspeth round His bed,
For this night God's voice hath said—
    " Seek the road that lieth nearest,
E'er the eastern sky is red."

3 "O my loved One ! " hear her cry,
    "Why should wicked men alarm Thee
Herod bids that Thou should'st die,
Soldiers stern in waiting lie,
    If they saw Thee could they harm Thee,
Thou, the Son of God most High ? "

4 Through black clouds the morning breaks;
    To her heart her Child she presseth:
E'er from baby sleep He wakes
Hurried flight towards Egypt takes,
    And the God of Israel blesseth
Who the lowly ne'er forsakes.

5 " Safe, oh safe," with joy she cries;
    " Safe from Herod's wrathful madness,"
Wide around the desert lies,
Quiv'ring under cloudless skies,
    God hath filled her heart with gladness
And her fear with darkness dies.

(4)

The Stars are bright.

HOLY INNOCENTS' DAY.

The stars are bright o'er Bethle - hem, As shine in

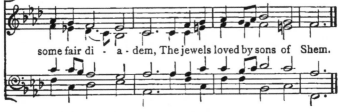

some fair di - a - dem, The jewels loved by sons of Shem.

2 But mothers weep in Bethlehem,
   As mothers wept in antient Kem,
   When God's dread angel passed o'er them.

3 For blood is sprinkled on the doors,
   And blood is darkening on the floors,
   And wrath, like Abel's blood, implores.

4 For he who weareth David's crown
   Hath trodden David's children down,
   And filled with wailing David's town.

5 Blest Innocents for Jesus' sake,
   Unwitting sacrifices make,
   And in good angels' arms awake.

6 And God Who wipeth tears away
   Hath placed them in the bright array
   Of those who praise Him night and day.

7 And mothers weeping children dead,
   Who died in their Redeemer's stead,
   By God Himself are comforted.

On this day was born.

CHRISTMAS DAY.

On this day was born Christ Je - sus, ve - ry ear - ly,
Shepherds watching by their sheepfolds, saw a wondrous

ere 'twas light,
vi - sion bright; For the gates of heav'n were o - pen'd,

and from out their por - tals fair, The an - gel - ic

song of se - raphs float - ed down the morn-ing air.

(6)

So for ever and for ever shall this Christmas Day be glad,
And with ivy and with holly are our homes and churches
clad;
Lordly palace, humble cottage, both alike are blithe and gay
For 'tis glory be to Jesus, Who was born on Christmas Day.

3.

In his palace sat King Herod, and his face was stern and
grim,
For there came three Eastern sages, and they wanted news
from him
Of a King all kings surpassing, for His star appeared to them,
And across the golden desert had they sought Jerusalem.

4.

Scribe and priest before King Herod straight their antient
scrolls unrolled,
And they found it had been written by prophetic seer of old
That in Bethlehem of Judah, of a Virgin should be born,
From the line of good King David, Christ to save this world
forlorn.

5.

Then rejoice with mage and shepherd, at the good news angels
bring,
Lift on high your alleluias, songs and carols let us sing;
Rich and poor, and young and aged, raise to heaven your
joyful lay,
For 'tis glory be to Jesus, Who was born on Christmas Day.

Glad hymns with one accord.

CHRISTMAS DAY.

Glad hymns with one ac - cord, We raise to Christ our Lord,

We praise His wondrous birth Who came from heav'n to earth,

And left His Fa -ther's throne To come un - to His own.

And all the world is gay, For Christ is born to - day.

2 E'en those who love Him not
   Good gifts from Him have got,
   For all, both good and bad
   At Christmas time are glad,
   E'en though no song of praise
   For His great love they raise.
   And all the world is gay,
   For Christ is born to-day.

3 From out the ice-bound north
   Glad songs are sounding forth.
   And torrid Asia's plain
   Takes up the gladsome strain,
   And ocean isles afar
   With us rejoicing are.
   And all the world is gay,
   For Christ is born to-day.

4 For God's great gift to men
   Let us do good again,
   And help the sick and sad,
   And make the mourners glad;
   And pray for those who fall
   To God Who loveth all.
   For all the world is gay,
   For Christ is born to-day.

5 Around us while we sing
   Are poised on noiseless wing,
   God's angel host unseen—
   High heaven and earth between;
   And in the music float
   Of tuneful organ note.
   For heaven and earth are gay,
   For Christ is born to-day.

Outside the city gates.

S. STEPHEN'S DAY.

Out - side the ci - ty gates .. an ea - ger crowd is wend - ing, With fran - tic rage pos - sessed, their gar-ments wild - ly rend - ing, And on - ly one is calm, .. his hands to heaven ex - tend - ing.

(10)

2.

And heeding not their rage, small care for life he taketh,
But with his dying breath a prayer for them he maketh,
As o'er his bloodstained face the light of morning breaketh.

3.

He sees beyond the stars, such sight was ne'er beholden
By mortal eyes before; he sees the portal golden
Of heaven, and angel hosts his wondering soul embolden.

4.

Such hosts as Jacob saw on Bethel's lofty ladder :—
On earth another host, than wolves of Edom madder,
When men for man's blood thirst, no sight on earth is sadder.

5.

He thinketh nought of earth, all heaven is shining o'er him ·
Nor word nor look for earth ; yet one who stands before him,
Whose eager face he scans, shall recompense restore him.

6.

But once their eyes have met, and yet that look for ever
Shall haunt the soul of Saul—to be forgotten never,
That " angel's face " from him, nor life, nor death shall sever.

7.

While Christmas songs are sung, and Christmas bells are
    swinging,
Comes Blessed Stephen's Day : thus pain with gladness
    mingling,
The world with echo faint, a dirge is vainly ringing.

On Asia Minor's sunny shore.

S. JOHN'S DAY.

On A·sia Mi·nor's sun·ny shore A ci·ty stood of won·drous fame. Of mar·ble reared by kings of yore To great . . Di·an·a's might·y name. . .

2 Where now the solemn sea-birds make
   'Mid reed and rush their silent home,
And jackals hungry wanderings take,
   As o'er the moonlit sands they roam.

3 But ere her lordliness was gone,
   And ere her royal temple fell,
There lived the blest Apostle John,
   Whom Jesus Christ had loved so well.

4 So old, a hundred winters' rime
   Had silvered o'er his snow-white hair ;
He seemed almost as old as Time,
   And yet he bore no marks of care.

5 His aged hands in some good deed
   Of charity and kindliness
Were active still where'er was need,
   And when they could not work would bless

6 Disciples crowded at his side,
   And evermore he told to them
How Jesus loved, and worked, and died,
   In desolate Jerusalem.

7 So, loved and loving till the last,
   At length he laid him down to rest ;
To Paradise he calmly past,
   Once more to lie on Jesu's breast.

Across the desert sands by night.

HOLY INNOCENTS' DAY.

A - cross the de - sert sands by night His
jour - ney Jo - seph tak - eth; At God's command his
has - ty flight; With an-xious speed he mak - eth, And
Beth - le - hem for - sak - eth.

2 For Herod seeks the child to slay
   And grudgeth e'en a manger,
Thus early Christ is driven away,
   A King, and yet a stranger ;
   A Babe, and yet in danger.

3 At Herod's court the noise is heard
   Of soldiers swiftly arming :
Have heralds come to bring him word
   Of night-attack alarming ?
   Of foes his country harming ?

4 He hears that Christ the King is born
   With craven fear he quaketh :
His armament God puts to scorn,
   Nor heeds the care he taketh,
   Nor heeds the speed he maketh.

5 But nought can harm that holy Child,
   For angels watch are keeping ;
And nought can harm that mother mild
   Who sadly goes and weeping,
   And folds her infant sleeping.

6 He slays the babes of Bethlehem,
   Her children, Rachel weepeth ;
But God great honour gives to them—
   Their souls He safely keepeth,
   Who slumbereth not nor sleepeth.

Price One Shilling.

A SELECTION OF
CHRISTMAS CAROLS

FROM THE COLLECTION EDITED BY

The Rev. H. R. BRAMLEY and Dr. STAINER,

ARRANGED FOR

MEN'S VOICES.

The growing use of Carols as open-air music on winter nights, when soprano voices, either of boys or women, are not easily obtained, has suggested the issue of the above, which includes twenty-four of the most popular Carols, old and new.

CONTENTS.

Price Two Shillings.

LONDON: NOVELLO AND COMPANY, LIMITED.

CHRISTMAS-TIDE CAROLS

(*SECOND SERIES*)

THE WORDS BY

Rev. BERNARD REYNOLDS

PREBENDARY OF S. PAUL'S

THE MUSIC

(Old French Melodies)

HARMONIZED BY

GEORGE C. MARTIN

ORGANIST OF S. PAUL'S CATHEDRAL.

Price ~~Sixpence~~ Eightpence.

WORDS ONLY, THREE HALF-PENCE.

LONDON: NOVELLO AND COMPANY, LIMITED.

NEW YORK: THE H. W. GRAY CO., SOLE AGENTS FOR THE U.S.A.

CHRISTMAS-TIDE CAROLS.

The Shepherds glad.

CHRISTMAS EVE.

The shepherds glad are on their way the ba - by King to greet, .. While back the an - gel host re - turns in ser - ried or - der meet; .. With count-less my - riad mov - ing wings the vault of heaven is dim. . . As

upward sweep triumphant hosts of radiant Se - ra - phim.

2.

And songs, more sweet than Jubal sang, around them echo far
Above the hills, above the clouds, above the morning star ;
So sweet, so glad, on Christmas morn—the jarring cries of sin
Unheard to joy-filled heaven arise, nor dare to enter in.

3.

A golden bridge of moving wings athwart the sky is seen,
As when the summer moonbeams paint the sleeping waves,
    with sheen ;
So shone the welcome rainbow round the Ark on Ararat,
So shone the bow that girt the throne whereon Jehovah sat.

4.

For evermore that bridge abides, uniting man with God,
And ever by the noiseless feet of passing souls is trod ;
Sweet souls, for whom the waves are calmed, for whom all
    tempests cease,
Who hear for aye the angels sing the songs of joy and peace.

Merrily ring the Christmas Bells.

CHRISTMAS EVE.

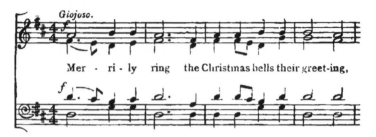

Mer - ri - ly ring the Christmas bells their greet-ing,

Mer - ri - ly friends are one an - o -ther meet - ing,

Glad - ly to one and all the Christmas news re - peat - ing.

Friends far away, whom half the world doth sever,
Friends far away, whom love forgetteth never,
Friends who will keep a place in anxious hearts for ever.

3.

Gladly with them we meet around the manger,
We in our peaceful homes—they girt by danger,
Where other brighter stars are shining o'er the stranger.

4.

Homeward and heav'nward, hearts to-day are turning,
Thoughts all of home in kindred souls are burning,
Who for our Christmas love in foreign lands are yearning.

5.

Joy on this day from all the world ascendeth,
Bridging the gulf that half the ocean rendeth,
Till o'er the earth shall break the song that never endeth

The sombre shadows darker fall.

CHRISTMAS EVE.

The som - bre sha - dows dark - er fall, Be - fore the morn - ing breaks : And jar -ring night-birds loud-er call, Ere day re - joic - ing wakes. So hearts of men wax'd cold, And sin and doubt more bold, Be -

- fore the   Christ-mas morn,   When Je-sus Christ was born.

2.

And ere the Christmas sun arose,
   Through towering heathen shrines,
Where Isis frowns in calm repose,
   Or jewelled Mithras shines:
      There rang, resounding clear,
      A voice that all might hear ;
      While priests their altars fled :
      " Great Pan is dead—is dead."

3.

But gladly woke the waiting earth,
   The birds more sweetly sang,
When heralding the glorious birth
   The angels' welcome rang :—
      The Sun hath risen at last,
      The darkness all is past,
      For 'tis the happy morn
      When Jesus Christ is born.

(9)

Poising bright on golden wing.

CHRISTMAS.

Soprano or Tenor Solo.

Pois-ing bright on gold-en wing, Angels from heaven sing,

Chorus.

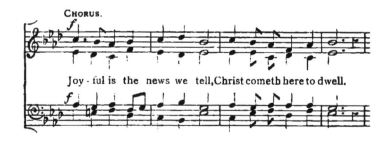

Joy - ful is the news we tell, Christ cometh here to dwell.

Solo.

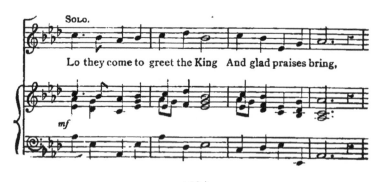

Lo they come to greet the King And glad praises bring,

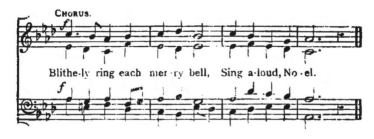

Blithe-ly ring each mer-ry bell, Sing a-loud, No-el.

2.

Solo. Prostrate low before them lies,
Death with his hollow eyes;

Chorus. Joyful is the news we tell,
Christ cometh here to dwell.

Solo. Sadness dull with pent-up sighs
Fast before them flies,

Chorus. Blithely ring each merry bell,
Sing aloud, Noel.

3.

Solo. All the world is bright and gay,
This merry Christmas Day;

Chorus. Joyful is the news we tell,
Christ cometh here to dwell.

Solo. Forth upon their joyous way
Now they speed for aye;

Chorus. Blithely ring each merry bell
Sing aloud, Noel.

(11)

Round the Virgin gently sleeping.

CHRISTMASTIDE.

Round the Vir-gin gen - tly sleep - ing, An- gels ga - ther all un - seen, Constant watch a - round her keep·ing, She of wo· man · kind the Queen. Ho-lier Eve, no E - den weep - ing, . . Fold-ing Christ her arms be - tween.

2.

Wondrous dreams those Angels brought her,
　　Such as mortals may not tell ;
Dreams which all the future taught her,
　　Such as greeted Israel.
She, great Israel's greater daughter,
　　She herself the true Bethel.

3.

Lo she looks adown the ages,
　　Sees adoring kings unborn ;
Hears the songs of babes and sages
　　Greet the ever-rising dawn ;
Whilst retreating darkness rages
　　Powerless o'er the conquering morn.

4.

Hears the Christmas song of gladness
　　Floating onwards round the world,
Easing grief and charming sadness,
　　Whilst the flag of God unfurled
Triumphs over Satan's madness—
　　Into outer darkness hurled.

5.

While she sleeps angelic blessing
　　Gilds the night with joyful ray ;
When she wakes, her Son's caressing
　　Hallows all the labouring day.
So from man all thoughts distressing
　　Christmas chases far away.

The Circumcision.

To - day the Sa - viour, eight . . days old, . . Was

nam ed . . as . the an - gel told,

All names a - bove is Je - su's name, Who

from His throne to save . us . . came.

Eight days of blessedness they were,
To Joseph pure, and unto her
Who gained the heavenly Paradise,
That Eve had lost through sin's device.

3.

Eight blessings for eight days they count,
As in the Sermon on the Mount ;
For shepherds " poor in spirit " first
Heard angel-songs o'er earth outburst.

4.

And mothers who their children ' mourn,'
Are blessed, though with anguish torn.
Most " meek," most blessed too is she
Who sang, " God magnifieth me."

5.

Of all who " hunger," all who " thirst
For righteousness," is he the first
Who " Nunc dimittis " sang at last
When unto God he calmly past.

6.

And " merciful " the Magi were
With gold and frankincense and myrrh.
Most " pure" was Joseph, Guardian blest
So stilly passing into rest.

7.

Of those who bring us " peace " the best
Is Christ, Who blesseth and is blest ;
And " persecution's " crown to gain
The babes of Bethlehem were slain.

In the golden lands afar.

EPIPHANY

In the golden lands a - far, Melchior, Gaspar, Balthasar

Saw the por-tent-bear-ing star Gild-ing all the hea-ven

With the light of se - ven. For - sak - ing their

lei-sure, O'er sands without measure They car-ry their trea-sure.

(16)

Kingly gifts their presents were,
Gold and frankincense and myrrh,
Gathered from the land of Ur.
    Gifts long stored and savèd
    For the Son of David.
Forsaking their leisure, &c.

3.

One was young and one was old,
One but half his life had told :
Passing dangers manifold,
    Where the white stars quiver
    In Euphrates' river.
Forsaking their leisure, &c.

4.

Till above them, towering high,
David's citadel they spy,
Glooming all the western sky :
    Scornfully upraising
    Giant walls amazing.
Forsaking their leisure, &c.

5.

Safe from Herod's impious guile,
Glozing them with cruel wile,
Guiding beams above them smile :
    Of the star resplendent
    Over Christ attendant.
Forsaking their leisure, &c.

6.

Now before Him worshipping—
Kingly gifts to greet a king
For the Gentile world they bring.
    Gifts of old appointed
    For the Lord's anointed.

A Legend of the Flight.

Allegretto.

In haste the dy - ing E - dom -ite his ar - my calls, From Teu - ton bri - gands gathered and from hea-then Gauls, And bids them slay The babes that play Round Rachel's honoured tomb to-day.

2.

But Joseph, warned of God, the Child and Mother takes,
And flying Herod's cruel wrath all speed he makes;
And through the night,
In anxious flight,
They journey till the morning light.

(18)

When lo! across their way an aged crone doth stand,
And bids them stay their onward flight with outstretched hand
"Ye wanderers three,
Come, list to me,
And ye shall all the future see.

4.

"Me Zingarella men do call, and bowing low,
The hidden future's teeming secrets think to know.
I pray ye stay,
And hear me say
What God hath taught to me this day.

5.

"On Judah's hills behold a cross upraised on high,
On which thy Son, the Son of God Himself must die.
His mother dear
Is standing near,
And all His woes doth see and hear.

6.

"But lo! above his lordly grave the morning breaks,
And over all the waking world triumphant makes
An endless dawn:
Thy Son is born,
Blest maid, to save a world forlorn.'

7.

And closer Mary folds her Babe within her breast,
And in His sleep by answering smile her love is blest:
And as they go,
Her joy doth show
Such peace as only mothers know.

Lightning Source UK Ltd.
Milton Keynes UK
UKHW010646090123
415051UK00006B/528